MW00747900

D-DAY
and the battle of Normandy

The fate of Europe was played out on the 6th of June 1944

On most of the monuments erected by the Comité du Débarquement along the Normandy coast appear the words "*Here, the Allied Forces liberated Europe*". But if in order to liberate Europe, it took the huge operation which the Normandy Landings constituted, the necessity for this dates back to 1940, when so much of Europe, including France, was occupied, something that had never before happened in history.

In 1940, as in 1944, it was Great Britain, the island neighbour of France, which performed the vital role because, in 1940, despite the heavy and sustained bombing of London and other cities, the Hurricane and Spitfire fighters of the R.A.F. and other Allied air forces engaged in the Battle of Britain destroyed so much of the Luftwaffe that German plans for an invasion had to be aborted. "Never in the field of human conflict has so much been owed by so many to so few".

At the same period, it was General de Gaulle who became the incarnation of France, eventually reasserting her legitimate place in history by virtue of the Republic which was re-established in Bayeux on the 14th June 1944. With the Free French, the Free Belgians, the Free Dutch, the Free Czechs and the Free Poles, Great Britain alone carried on the struggle until Russia was attacked in June 1941 and there occurred the decisive entry into the War of the United States of America, at the end of that year.

In part because of the geographical shape of France, with coastlines on several seas and with borders with so many other countries, it was natural that France should be the centre of operations, just as she had been in the First World War, and that two separate landings would be required. The first of these, in Normandy, was the decisive one, but all the same, Fate was needed to play its fullest part in favour of the Allies, because Hitler had secretly been developing weapons capable of annihilating not only London, but also all Southern Great Britain, where the Allied invasion forces were concentrated. In addition to the V1s and V2s, he had installed long-range gun batteries, or V3s, on the coast of the Pas-de-Calais, able to bombard the British coast. Had the date for the invasion been postponed any longer, Hitler's plans might have succeeded. But Eisenhower, the Supreme Commander and a great friend of France, decided after 24 hours of hesitation due to adverse weather conditions, to seize the window of opportunity presented by the forecast of a slight improvement in the weather, to launch the invasion on the 6th June, whereas 24 hours earlier, he had all but decided to defer it for a month.

On Hitler's side, sabotage by the Resistance prevented the V3 gun batteries from being able to fire until a month after D-Day.

In Normandy, the Resistance had been supplying the Allies with valuable intelligence on the German forces and had previously received the order that in the event of an invasion they were to frustrate, by any and every means at their disposal, German access to the coast. So it was that counter attacks by German armour on the 7th and 9th of June were only successful at two points on the coast, where isolated Allied units were unable to hold on to their positions.

One can indeed say that Europe deserved that Fate should be on its side during the Liberation.

Raymond TRIBOULET
Ex-Minister
Member of the Institut de France
Founder of the Comité du Débarquement

THE DECISION TO INVADE

From June 1940 onwards, following Dunkirk and before the capitulation of France, Churchill realised that to defeat Hitler it would be necessary to invade the Continent.

By the end of June 1940, only Great Britain, with a few contingents of volunteers from other occupied countries, among whom were the Free French, remained at War with Germany, but with an Army that had urgently to be rebuilt. During these few months after the defeat on the Continent, two fundamental concepts were formulated:
- To return in force to the Continent,
- To give priority to the defeat of Germany.

The invasion of the Soviet Union in June 1941 was to give a special emphasis to the development of these concepts.

At the Washington meeting of December 1941, following Pearl Harbour, Roosevelt confirmed his priority: "*In spite of the entry of Japan into the War, Germany remains the main enemy and its defeat is the key to victory. When Germany is defeated, the collapse of Italy and Japan will follow*".

In April 1942, at the General Staff conference in London, Roosevelt's advisor and the Chief of Staff of the American Army were given the tasks of drawing up plans for the re-entry into Europe and of implanting American forces in Great Britain for the purpose of sharing in the struggle in Europe. In 1942, at the Churchill-Roosevelt conference in the USA, it was agreed that it was impossible to open a Second Front in Europe during 1943.

The "Quadrant" Conference in Quebec, August 1943.
Roosevelt, Churchill, surrounded by the members of the Combined Chiefs of staff (CCS).

The atmosphere was one of one of near crisis, but the situation was fortunately transformed by the stunning American naval victory of Midway and Roosevelt was able to confirm the priority given to defeating Germany.

In January 1942, following the American invasion of North Africa, Roosevelt and Churchill met in Casablanca. The decisions taken there marked a decisive step in planning of the opening of the Second Front in Europe. Among the measures taken, the two leaders decided to bring about, during 1943, all the preliminary conditions required for the execution of a landing on the continent of Europe in 1944.

The Casablanca Conference added a declaration of principal to the concrete decisions it took, namely: *"The War will be pursued until the Unconditional Surrender of the Hostile Powers is achieved"*.

Following the Casablanca Conference, the preliminary conditions for a landing; freedom of the seas and strategic bombing, would be studied and pursued by the Allied Combined Chiefs of Staff. Preparations for the landings themselves would be entrusted to a specially created Anglo-American General Staff.

THE MISSION :

To secure on European soil the necessary space to lead later to offensive action.

With this objective, to seize ports capable of permitting the arrival of reinforcements coming direct from the United States (at a rate of 3 to 5 Divisions per month), to back up the British and Canadian forces already on the ground.

Date of the objective: may 1944
Plans to be presented by 1st August 1943
Assault forces: 29 Divisions (plus 1 probable French Division), of which 5 + 2 Divisions in the initial assault and immediate reinforcements of 2 Divisions.

Once these initial studies were concluded, COSSAC decided on Lower Normandy as the site of the landings and at the Quebec Conference in August 1943, Roosevelt and Churchill and their advisors and Chiefs of Staff approved the COSSAC proposals. They ordered COSSAC to proceed straight away with the planning and preparation of Overlord. As a result, COSSAC became operational and during the second half of 1943, preparations for Overlord went full steam ahead.

On 25th May 1942, COSSAC (Chief of Staff to the Supreme Allied Commander) received from the Combined Chiefs of Staff a supplementary directive concerning Overlord. Concurrent to the amphibious operations conducted on the African and Mediterranean coasts, the idea of a landing operation in France was starting to take shape. In April 1943, the inter-Allied staff, the COSSAC, placed under General Morgan's command, set to elaborating the plans of this extremely complex military undertaking. In August the same year, Morgan's plan was presented at the Quadrant conference in Quebec. Soon to be baptised Overlord, the plan was approved by the Allied political and military bodies. The landings were to take place in Normandy, D-Day being scheduled for the 1st of May 1944.

THE COMMAND OF OVERLORD

STRATEGY

The first adversary to be over-thrown was in Europe, so it was in Europe that the efforts of the three allies, the Soviet Union, Great Britain and America had to be concentrated. Accordingly, the Operational Division, commanded by Eisenhower, decided on the necessity for a crossing of the Channel, in force, from bases set up in England. The criterion for the success of such an operation lay in the achievement of over-whelming air superiority.

In June 1942, President Roosevelt, convinced of the soundness of this strategic approach, appointed Eisenhower to take command of the American Forces in Europe which were then being created.

Eisenhower, officially designated Supreme Commander of the Allied Expeditionary Forces in Europe on the eve of Christmas 1943, took command of the Supreme Headquarters of Allied Expeditionary Forces (SHAEF) in London on the 15th of January 1944. He was then 49.

He had recently commanded the Allied landings in North Africa and had displayed a shrewd tactical sense and firm but unconfrontational qualities of leadership. He was at the peak of his powers. As head of his General Staff, he appointed the very efficient and forceful General Bedell Smith.

Appointed as Commander of the Naval forces was Admiral Ramsay, and as Commander of the Air forces, Air Marshal Leigh-Mallory, a veteran of the Battle of Britain. As his deputy, Eisenhower chose Marshal of the R.A.F. Tedder, whilst his Land force Commanders were Generals Montgomery and Bradley.

SUPREME HEADQUARTERS ALLIED EXPEDITIONARY FORCES
6th June 1944

General Dwight D. Eisenhower
Supreme Commander of the Allied Expeditionary Forces

Marshal of the R.A.F. Sir Arthur Tedder
Deputy Supreme Commander

General Walter Bedell-Smith
Chief of Staff to the Supreme Commander

Admiral Sir Bertram H. Ramsay
Commander of the Naval forces

Marshal Sir Trafford Leigh-Mallory
Commander of the Air forces

General Sir Bernard Law Montgomery
Commander of the XXIst Army
Commander of the Land forces

 Marshal de l'air Sir Arthur Coningham
2nd Tactical Air Force

 General Lewis Brereton
9th US Airforce Tactical and Strategic Air forces

General Sir Miles Dempsey
Commander Britis IInd Army

General Omar Bradley
Commander American 1st Army

Admiral Alan G. Kirk
Tactical Naval forces West

Admiral Sir Philip L. Vian
Tactical Naval forces East

General Gérard Bucknall
Commander Br. 30th Corps GOLD

General J.T Crocker
Commander Br. 1st Corps GOLD and JUNO

General Lawton Collins
Commander Am. 7th Corps UTAH

General Léonard T. Gerow
Commander Am. 5th Corps OMAHA

Beginning of August 1944

General Dwight D. Eisenhower

 General Sir Bernard Law Montgomery
British XXIst Army Group

General Omar Bradley
American 11th Army Group

General Sir Miles Dempsey
British IInd Army

General Henry D. Crerar
Canadian 1st Army

General Courtney Hicks Hodges
American 1st Army

General George S. Patton
Commander American 3th Army

7th Corps G.B.

30th Corps G.B

12th Corps G.B.

2nd Corps Canadien

1st Corps G.B.

7th Corps U.S.

19th Corps U.S.

5th Corps U.S.

8th Corps U.S.

20th corps U.S.

15th corps U.S.

12th corps U.S.

DECEPTION OPERATIONS

Plan 'Fortitude', put into operation in September 1943, had the objective of creating in the German High Command the element of surprise so vital to an Allied success by concealing the truth and inducing the enemy to believe in false information. The truth was difficult to conceal, given the formidable concentration of land, naval and air forces in and around the British Isles which German air reconnaissance could hardly fail to detect, despite the fact that the Allies were well on the way to achieving complete mastery of the air. The dispersion of war material throughout Britain and in all its ports, demanded by the sheer magnitude of the forces being assembled, made it difficult for the enemy to determine the direction in which a future attack might take place. However, in the final weeks and days before D-Day, the increased activity in ports in the South West of England had to be disguised by an equivalent, but dissimulated, activity along the East coast. This was done.

In the same way, radio traffic was kept at the same level in the South East as in the South West so that the density of the traffic alone, without even any decipherment of the signals, would not provide any clues to the German listening posts. This camouflage of the real intentions was maintained right up to the landings. During the night the landing forces set sail for Normandy, 105 R.A.F. planes and 34 small Royal Navy craft operated continually in the Channel on both side of the port of Boulogne, releasing balloons and dropping chaff, causing overloading of the German listening stations and radars in the Pas-de-Calais.

These protective measures were reinforced by steps to saturate the German intelligence services with spurious intelligence information; false news was leaked to neutral journalists and diplomats in England. The Allied Intelligence Services surpassed themselves; in May 1944 a double of General Montgomery was ostentatiously welcomed in Gibraltar so as to give credibility to the idea that a landing was being planned for Spain or in Southern France, an idea which was speedily transmitted to Berlin by the many Germans living in Spain.

During June and July 1944, the threat of a second landing in the Pas-de-Calais area was sustained by assembling a fleet of old barges in the South East of England and by artificially creating the tracks of armoured vehicles in the sand of the beaches in this area, often the object of German reconnaissance planes. In the same way, the American General Patton, well-known and much feared by the Germans, but

held in reserve by General Eisenhower until July 1944, frequently visited the Dover area. These visits were well-publicised, so that they led the Germans to believe that under his command, a second landing would take place in the North of France.

Dummy tanks and other equipment, made of plywood, fabric and rubber, were constructed and sited as decoys to deceive the enemy.

On 5ᵗʰ June 1944, General Eisenhower prepares his parachute forces for combat.

PREPARATIONS FOR THE ASSAULT

At the Quebec conference in August 1943, the Allied civilian and military authorities were first informed of the plans for a large-scale landing on the European continent. The project was code-named Overlord and envisaged the huge enterprise of landing large armies on terra firma taking place without the use of a continental port.

After revision, the COSSAC plan provided for an assault on a front of 40km, carried out by an Army Corps of 3 Divisions, followed by 3 Corps of immediate reinforcements, each of 3 Divisions, plus 1 to 2 Divisions of airborne troops, with the means of landing these forces (6,047 landing craft). The desired invasion force would thus involve the following: 176,500 men and 20,000 vehicles (including 3,000 guns, 1,500 tanks and 5,000 armoured vehicles) to be landed within the first 48 hours of the initial invasion.

On D-Day, Eisenhower commanded a force without parallel in history.
- 37 Divisions on British soil which, having landed in France, would be joined by 50 Divisions arriving direct from the United States.
- A fleet of warships numbering 1,000 ships.
- An airforce comprising 10,000 planes.

Once all the required studies had taken place, it was decided that the assault should take place on the date of the highest half-tide at the most Westerly beach (Utah), 40 minutes after first light and following a night when the moon rose between 1 and 2 am. Such occasions occur 3 times each month and in June 1944, they represented the 5ᵗʰ, 6ᵗʰ and 7ᵗʰ of that month.

As the date of the landings grew nearer, the naval plan "Neptune" was put into operation; 5 naval forces, corresponding to the 5 chosen landing beaches on the Normandy coast, were assembled. Some figures illustrate the enormous dimensions of the invasion to be launched on 6th June and the size of the supporting forces involved. 5,000 naval ships and 2,000 additional vessels (employed to ferry men and supplies from ship to shore). The main naval force consisted of 6 battleships, 2 monitors, 22 cruisers and 93 torpedo boats.

The role of the Resistance must not be overlooked. Before Overlord, opportunities open to the Resistance were:
- action to obstruct the means of communication.
- the supply of military intelligence.

By the evening of the 3rd of June, everything was ready for an airborne assault on the nights of 4th or 5th June, plus an amphibious assault on the 5th at 06.30 hours.

Then began the drama of the weather. From the 1st of June, weather conditions dete-rio-rated, with strong winds and a rough sea. While the naval force 'U' was already at sea, at 03.00 hours the meteorologists announced a worsening of the weather during the forthcoming days. Any delay in launching the invasion would be serious and cause terrible congestion in the ports. It would hardly be possible to keep the planned invasion a secret. In any case, during June, only the 5th, 6th or 7th were feasible dates.

Eisenhower put off that part of the operation planned for the 4th until the 5th. Although part of the fleet was a sea and the cancellation order had been given, he decided to launch the invasion on the 6th and kept the fleet at sea, which confused Rommel On the morning of the 5th, the chief meteorologist announced an unexpected weather change for the night of 5th/6th, with calmer seas for some hours until around the evening of the 6th, and with less wind and better visibility.

Eisenhower decides that "Overlord will take place on the 6th of June". Eisenhower could then do little other than allow the scenario prepared, under his orders, with such infinite care and precision for 4 months, to take its course. On the afternoon of the 5th, he visited the parachutists of the 82nd and 101st Airborne Divisions which were to carry out, that night, a mission which, in his view, would be crucial to the success of the invasion. "Les sanglots longs des violons d'automne blessent mon cœur d'une langueur monotone" This, the second part of a strophe by Verlaine was broadcast by the BBC on the 5th June, at 20.15 hours, to tell the Resistance that the invasion had been launched.

OPERATION NEPTUNE

Under the command of Admiral Ramsay, Operation Neptune was responsible for the passage from one side of the Channel to the other of the huge number of men and the enormous mass of equipment which, for nearly two years, had been increasingly overloading the space available in the British Isles. One thousand naval ships, troop transports, and a myriad of landing craft, transported the 132,000 men comprising the first wave of the assault force and all their equipment.

Sailing from many ports in Southern England, but mainly from Portsmouth, 5,000 vessels came together, early at night, at a rendez-vous in mid-Channel designated zoneZ, but given the nickname 'Piccadilly Circus' because of the congestion caused by the almost unbelievable number of ships assembled there.

Zone Z had been chosen so as to leave the Germans in doubt for as long as possible as to where the assault was to take place: would it be Normandy or the Pas-de-Calais?

Along previously dredged channels, the five naval forces allocated to the five beaches then set sail;
- 2 Americans, to the West
- 2 British and 1 Canadian, to the East

82nd Airborne

Cherbourg
Montebourg

101st Airborne

Sainte-Mère-Église

Carentan

Bayeux

101st Airborne

Saint-Lô

Caen

6th June 1944, 00.15 hours

The parachute landing of the first scouts.

DIVISIONS

82nd Division: Commander Major General M.B. Ridgway
101st Division : Commander Major General M.D. Taylor

MISSION

- To seize Ste-Mère-Eglise
- Cut the R.N. 13 linking Cherbourg and Paris
- Establish a bridgehead on the West bank of the Merderet and prevent its being crossed by the Germans
- Prevent any attack on Ste-Mère-Eglise
- Control the coast where the naval landing had already begun.

UTAH BEACH

The airborne troops

Each Division was a force of some 7,000 men, comprising 3 Regiments plus communications teams, medical services and 200 infantrymen per Division, all arriving in gliders with their war material. 1,662 aircraft and 512 gliders were deployed for this Operation. A single DC3 (C.47) aircraft carried between 25 and 30 parachutists.

The parachutists were dropped in successive waves, but their formations, hampered by anti-aircraft fire, cloud and poor radio communications, became scattered. Some units landed in the sea and others behind enemy lines. Moreover, the terrain, comprising thick hedges and artificially flooded areas in the area of the Merderet, added to the troops' difficulties.

In spite of heavy casualties (2,500 men of the two Divisions), most of the vital missions were successfully accomplished. Overall, the operation was a success.

Flooded areas and thick hedges added to the difficulties.

Model figure suspended from the bell tower of Ste-Mère-Eglise church in memory of John Steele who suffered this sad fate.

The Infantry

While the parachutists were attempting to regroup in the labyrinth of hedgerows and marshland of Normandy, the transportation of troops in landing craft went ahead without hindrance. Forty minutes before Zero Hour, the guns of the naval vessels opened up and the 276 attack aircraft of the 9th U.S. Airforce went into action.

The assault on UTAH consisted of 4 waves:
- **The first wave** comprised 20 LCPVs each with a team of 30 men.
- **The second wave** numbered 32 LCPVs with the remainder of the two assault battalions, some Engineers and 8 teams of Marine Sappers.
- **The third wave**, timed to land at 15 minutes after Zero Hour, comprised 8 LCTs loaded with bulldozer tanks. This wave was to be followed 2 minutes later by the fourth wave mainly composed of detachments of the 237th and 299th Battalions of Engineers, responsible for clearing the beaches.

By the end of the day, the 4th Division had attained almost all its objectives. 23,250 men, 17,000 vehicles and 1,695 tons of supplies had been landed.

6th June 1944, 06.30 hours

Off the beach of La Madeleine

DIVISIONS

4th Infantry Division
Commander:
Major General R.D. Barton

MISSION

- To join up with the 101st Airborne Division

- Establish a bridgehead around the area of Quinéville, Ste-Mère-Eglise, Ste-Marie-du-Mont

- To join up with the 82nd Division near the river Merderet

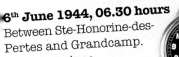

6th June 1944, 06.30 hours
Between Ste-Honorine-des-Pertes and Grandcamp.
(Rangers since 04.30 hours)

DIVISIONS

1st Infantry Division
Commander :
Major General C.R. Huebner
29th Infantry Division
Commander :
Major General C.H. Gerhardt

MISSION

• To seize the access roads to the interior and reach the line Isigny, Trévières, Vaucelles.

• For the 116th Regiment, to capture the 6-gun battery at La Pointe du Hoc. Two Battalions of Rangers were to support this operation.

OMAHA BEACH

Omaha this is the name of a town in the Nebraska, in the United States, on the Missouri River and it was given as the code-name for one of the landing beaches. This major assault force met with fire from automatic weapons and the artillery of the German 716th and 352nd Divisions.

At the epicentre of a front extending from Utah in the West and Gold in the East, this landing zone was one of the most exposed because backed by rocky cliffs and strong defences.

On a barrier of concrete 'Dragon's Teeth', supposedly impossible to cross, and for hours without interruption, was poured an unparalleled volume of enemy fire. Nevertheless, at the cost of heavy losses of human life, it was crossed and then, successive waves of men, subjected to mortal hazards, followed on without let up.

Many of these brave units were decimated by the deadly fire from the blockhouses and dugin batteries. Against all odds, others took the place of the fallen and opened up the first ways through the soil of France. Omaha will always bear the name of "Omaha the bloody".

By the end of this day, 34,500 men had been landed and a small bridgehead 1 to 2km in depth and 7km wide had been created. Of the 2,400 tons of supplies which should have been landed, only 100 tons arrived safely. Almost all the artillery, most of the tanks and the means of transport had been engulfed by the sea. Munitions were in short supply. Official figures indicated over 4,000 American dead or wounded.

LA POINTE DU HOC

Half-way between Omaha and Utah, La Pointe du Hoc dominates the sea because of its vertical cliffs. It was topped by a heavy gun battery protected by concrete bunkers. These batteries had to be taken in order to free the beaches from the danger they represented. Such was the mission entrusted to 225 Rangers of the 2nd Battalion, commanded by Lieut.-Colonel Rudder.

American cemetery at Colleville St Laurent.

On previous days, La Pointe du Hoc had been the target of heavy bombing attacks and unknown to the Rangers, the 155mm guns had been withdrawn and sited further to the rear.

By 07.00 hours, the Rangers had reached to top of the cliff, access to which was covered by German fire from a fortified house. Using firemen's ladders, fitted to barges, ropes and grapnels fired from rifles and mortars, the Rangers climbed the cliff without too many casualties and took up their positions, having overcome the enemy resistance. However, counter-attacks by a greatly numerically-superior

The remains of the German defences at La Pointe du Hoc.

enemy, determined to eliminate the Rangers, caused heavy losses among the 3 isolated Companies of Rangers who had suffered losses and were running short of ammunition.

On the morning of the 7th, the strength of the units on the Pointe was down to only 90 or 100 men capable of fighting and many of these had been slightly wounded. They had no food, were low in ammunition, and were pinned down in the ruins of the enemy fortifications which had been destroyed.

In the morning of the 8th, in a concerted attack by the 5th Rangers and the 1st Battalion of the 116th Infantry Regiment and the 3rd Battalion, plus 5 tanks and backed by fire from the destroyer Ellyson, La Pointe du Hoc was cleared. Colonel Rudder rubs his face and straightens up on his feet; he was exhausted and the price of the fearful casualties his Battalion had suffered weighed heavily on his broad shoulders.

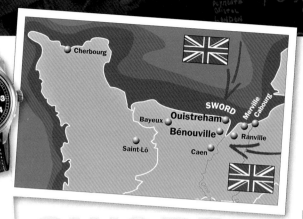

**6th June 1944,
00.15 hours**
The first gliders

DIVISIONS

6th British Airborne Division, with 2 Brigades (the 5th and 3rd included a Canadian Parachute Battalion)
Commander :
Major General R. Gale

MISSION

- To seize the bridges over the Caen Canal at Bénouville and over the Orne at Ranville
- Exclude access to the area between the Orne and the Dives
- Destroy 5 designated bridges
- Neutralise the gun battery at Merville

SWORD BEACH

The airborne troops

Of the 6 gliders released a few minutes after midnight, three landed close to the Benouville bridge. Within a short time, the German defenders were overcome. Two other gliders landed near the Ranville bridge and the last one got lost 14 kilometres away. The bridge was rapidly seized.

Before daybreak on D-Day all the missions allocated to the 6th Airborne Division had been achieved, but numerous parachutists had gone missing in the flooded areas on both side of the river Dives and a large proportion of the equipment was lost. The neutralisation of the Merville battery caused heavy losses and casualties for the whole operation were estimated to be 600 killed or wounded, 600 missing and about 100 glider pilots killed, wounded or missing.

Synchronising watches before H-Hour.

Gliders landing close to "Pegasus Bridge".

The bridge over the Caen Canal at Bénouville today

The Infantry

General Rennie, commanding the 3rd Division, was less worried about the resistance that the weak German 716th Infantry Division might put up than he was about the possibility of a counter attack by the 21st Panzer Division, stationed South of Caen, should this take place before he could firmly establish his Division on Norman soil and be able to withstand an attack. It was precisely to counter this danger that General Gale's 6th Airborne Division was landed during the night on the East of the Orne and was widely dispersed between Troarn and the Dives. Shortly before midnight, it seized the vital bridge at Benouville. When the 3rd Division landed, General Gale set up his headquarters at Ranville, 3km East of this bridge. In spite of the problems caused by the swell, tanks and infantry landed at Sword in the face of resistance largely neutralised by exceptionally heavy and effective prior bombardment.

At 09.30 hours, Hermanville was taken. At the same time, fighting took place to clear the region around Ouistreham where the French Commando under Commandant Kieffer had landed. Disembarking at the breach in the defences at ColleviLe-sur-Orne, which has since been renamed Colleville-Montgomery, the 177 French riflemen carried out their mission successfully. Their task was to take the fortified position at Riva-Bella, to clear Ouistreham and to link up with the airborne troops at Benouville; this they did around 12.30 hours.

Only at the beginning of the afternoon, because of the delay in unloading tanks onto a congested beach which was still being laboriously cleared by the Sappers, did fighting began to take the hill at Periers, from the summit of which Caen was visible. While the road to Caen appeared to be open, the British were to engage in a decisive battle with the 21st Panzer Division. Thanks to the Allied aerial superiority which gave them complete mastery of the skies, the German reserves were unable to arrive until late at night, short of fuel and without any possibility of being resupplied.

Delayed in breaking out of the beachheads, held up by the prolonged resistance of some fortified emplacements on the coast and in the interior and finally by the counter attack of the 21st Panzer Division, nevertheless, the 3rd Division established a solid bridgehead, but Caen, which had been so nearly reached, did not fall until the 9th of July. Before midnight, 28,845 men had been landed. Losses were estimated to be 630 dead or wounded on the beach alone.

6th June 1944, 07.30 hours

The first landings between Lion-sur-Mer and Ouistreham

DIVISIONS

3rd British Infantry Division
Commander :
Major General T.G. Rennie

MISSION

• To capture Caen
• Establish liaison with the 6th Airborne Division

JUNO

JUNO BEACH

On Juno beach, the task of the 3rd Canadian Division was complicated by the presence of offshore shoals and by a heavy sea. In addition, some tanks were only beached with some delay. Hard-fought battles ensued between Courseulles and Bernieres, opening up breaches in the defences through which the tanks gave close support to the infantry and provided accurate fire.

6th June 1944, 08.00 hours

The first landings between Gray-sur-Mer and Bernières-sur-Mer

DIVISIONS

3e Canadian Infantry Division
Commander:
General R.H.L Keller.
2e Canadian armored Division
Commander:
Sergeant R.A.Wiyman.
48 Commando Royal Marines,

MISSION

• To seize a bridgehead 18km in depth, comprising the heights to the West of Caen ont the line Port-en-Bessin, Carpiquet.

• For 48 Commando (Royal Marines) to take the whole of the shore defences up to Langrune.

At 09.30 hours Bernieres was cleared of the last German resistance and progress Southwards commenced. Despite initial difficulties caused by the very bad weather, by the end of the day it was the Canadian Division which was closest to reaching the planned objectives.

The bridgehead extended to 10 to 12km in depth: and a junction being made to the West with the 50th division, the two bridgeheads were amalgamated. Caen was in sight. Two Battalions were within 5km of the town and in places, armour had reached the Caen-Bayeux road, but being isolated and without infantry support, it had to withdraw.

Delayed from the start by the state of the sea, submerged obstacles, the difficulty in creating openings and the congestion thus produced, as well as the opposition offered by the strong points which were still intact at Bernieres and St-Aubin, the Division was the only Allied unit to have reached its objectives without being able to hold them. However, it did hold a fairly well advanced line towards the interior. Liaison was established with the 50th Division (Gold), but this was not achieved with the British 3rd Division (Sword), since between the two was a wide gap.

21,400 men were landed as well as 3,200 vehicles and 1,100 tons of supplies. The human cost was 304 dead, 574 wounded and 47 taken prisoner.

The landing of Canadian units at Juno.

GOLD BEACH

Gold beach, at the centre of the landing zones, half-way between the Cotentin peninsular and the Orne, on either side of Asnelles, is enclosed and flanked by steep cliffs.

The task of the 50th Division therefore appeared difficult, despite all the prior preparations which were, as in this case, and at all the other beaches, air bombardments during the second part of the night, and at daybreak, naval gunfire continued right up to the moment of the assault on the beach.

Accompanied and supported by flail tanks and DD tanks which sometimes went ahead of the infantry, the British Brigades arrived at La Riviere and Le Hamel at 07.30 hours, progressively destroying blockhouses and German-built obstacles as they went.

By the evening, the 50th Division's bridgehead measured 10km by 10km and touched Bayeux, and also had the Bayeux-Caen road in its sights, a road which was vital for the German reserves.

The command post at Longues-sur-Mer.

The Brigade made contact with the 3rd Canadian Division on its left flank. However, it had not reached all its objectives for D-Day, nor ensured a link up with the Americans in the West.

24,970 men were landed. 89 barges or other craft were lost. On the beach alone, 413 men were either killed, wounded or missing.

By midnight, 2,500 obstacles met with on the 5km of beach, mostly mines, had been neutralised.

6th June 1944, 07.30 hours

Arrival of the first Brigades around Ver-sur-Mer and Asnelles.

DIVISIONS

50th Infantry Division
Commander:
Major General D.H.A. Graham

MISSION

• To seize the beach defensive positions

• Reach the R.N. 13 and take Bayeux

• Ensure liaison with the 3rd Canadian Infantry Division to the East, and the American troops at Omaha in the West

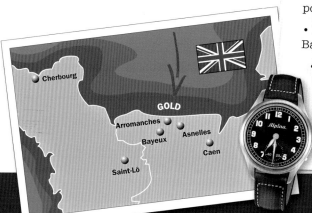

CARTOGRAPHY

Operation Neptune

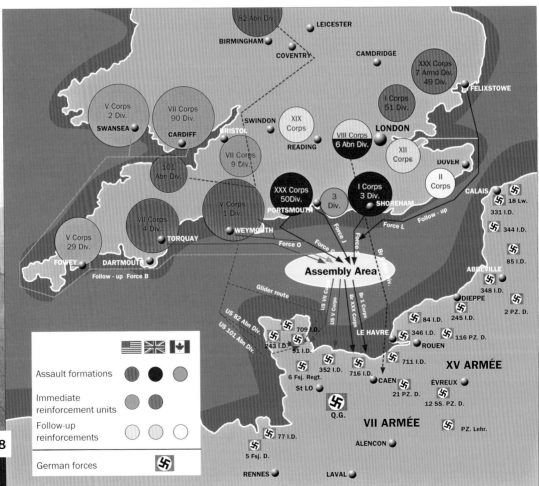

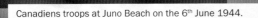

Canadiens troops at Juno Beach on the 6th June 1944.

The Battle of Normandy

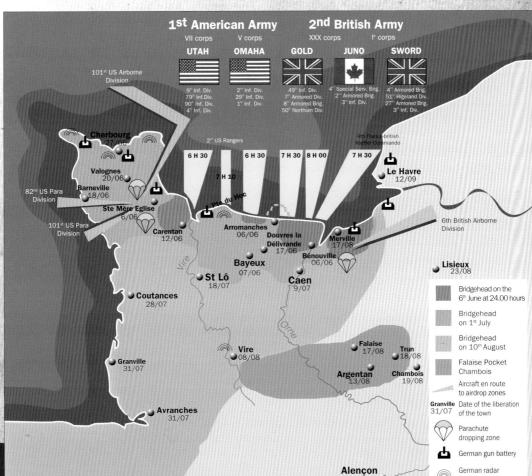

1st American Army		2nd British Army		
VII corps	V corps	XXX corps	I corps	
UTAH	OMAHA	GOLD	JUNO	SWORD
9th Inf. Div.	2nd Inf. Div.	49th Inf. Div.	4th Special Serv. Brig.	4th Armored Brig.
79th Inf.Div.	29th Inf. Div.	7th Armored Div.	2nd Armored Brig.	51th Higeland Div.
90th Inf. Div.	1st Inf. Div.	8th Armored Brig.	3rd Inf. Div.	27th Armored Brig.
4th Inf. Div.		50th Northum Div.		3rd Inf. Div.

101st US Airborne Division

2nd US Rangers

4th Franco-british Kieffer Commando

6 H 30   6 H 30   7 H 30   8 H 00   7 H 30

7 H 10

Cherbourg 27/06

Valognes 20/06

82nd US Para Division

Barneville 18/06

Ste Mère Eglise 6/06

101st US Para Division

Pte du Hoc

Carentan 12/06

Arromanches 06/06

Douvres la Délivrande 17/06

Merville 17/08

Bénouville 06/06

Le Havre 12/09

6th British Airborne Division

Lisieux 23/08

Bayeux 07/06

St Lô 18/07

Caen 9/07

Coutances 28/07

Vire 08/08

Falaise 17/08

Trun 18/08

Granville 31/07

Argentan 13/08

Chambois 19/08

Avranches 31/07

Alençon 12/08

Bridgehead on the 6th June at 24.00 hours

Bridgehead on 1st July

Bridgehead on 10th August

Falaise Pocket Chambois

Aircraft en route to airdrop zones

Granville 31/07 — Date of the liberation of the town

Parachute dropping zone

German gun battery

German radar station

19

THE PREFABRICATED HARBOURS

Map of the Arromanches Mulberry harbour

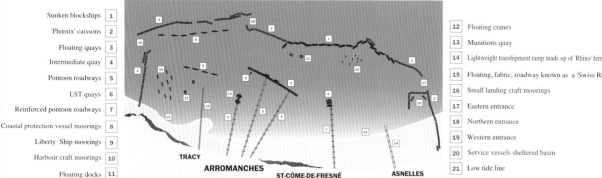

Sunken blockships	1
'Phœnix' caissons	2
Floating quays	3
Intermediate quay	4
Pontoon roadways	5
LST quays	6
Reinforced pontoon roadways	7
Coastal protection vessel moorings	8
Liberty Ship moorings	9
Harbour craft moorings	10
Floating docks	11

12	Floating cranes
13	Munitions quay
14	Lightweight transhipment ramp made up of 'Rhino' ferri
15	Floating, fabric, roadway known as a 'Swiss Ro
16	Small landing craft moorings
17	Eastern entrance
18	Northern entrance
19	Western entrance
20	Service vessels sheltered basin
21	Low tide line

Pending the liberation and restoration of the ports in the area of the landings (notably Cherbourg, Le Havre and Rouen) the creation of artificial roads and the placing of prefabricated quays and harbour installations was undertaken the day following D-Day.

Gooseberries: These were old merchant ships, sailed across the Channel and scuttled to form outer breakwaters offshore of the Utah, Omaha, Gold, Juno and Sword beaches so as to shelter the roads which they formed.

Mulberries: Offshore of Saint-Laurent (Omaha) and Arromanches (Gold) chains of huge concrete caissons (called Phoenix) were sunk into position to form artificial quays and provide sheltered roads. Prefabricated in Great Britain, and towed across the Channel, these units were sunk within little more than 30 minutes by opening valves to let in the sea. Within the breakwater so constructed, an ingenious system of floating quays, pontoon bridges/roadways, etc., allowed the rapid unloading of the transports tied up alongside. During the great storm of the 19th June, the Mulberries were severely damaged and the small harbour of Saint-Laurent was completely wrecked and had to be abandoned. Only the Arromanches Mulberry was able to be restored to use during the following days

Floating pontoon roadways.

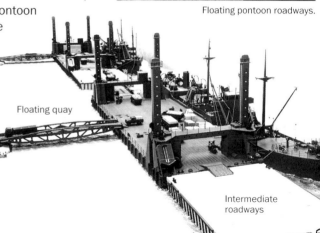

Floating quay

Intermediate roadways

The Allies had set foot on the Continent, opening a breach in the German defensive system known as the "Atlantic Wall". The Germans were taken by surprise; their communications networks disrupted. Nevertheless, all the Allied objectives had not been achieved and it was clear that the Battle of Normandy would be a hard-fought struggle. The courage displayed by the German soldiers presaged hard battles and great loss of life. It was essential to enlarge the bridgehead established by the evening of D-Day.

The objectives of the first day, the taking of Caen, the airfield at Carpiquet, remained unattained. German resistance would be very strong and Caen would only fall into British hands on the 9th of July. Cherbourg, the port which needed to be captured to provide the logistic base for the evolution of the battle, was only taken on 27th of June, after a long and hard fight. Only after these objectives had been attained could Eisenhower, Montgomery and Bradley plan to break out in the direction of the ports in Brittany and the North-East of France. The delay in resupplying the forces on the ground, due to adverse weather conditions, coupled with the tenacious German resistance in the Bocage, meant that it was the end of July before the ground forces could end their war of attrition and go on the offensive. This offensive, which was to end on the 20th June by the sealing off of the famous Falaise pocket, marked the end of the Battle of Normandy. Thereafter, the road to the Seine and Paris would be open.

In the battles which followed the landings on the 6th of June, one can identify three phases between that date and the 31st of July, the date on which began the operations that settled the fate of the German forces engaged in Normandy.
• The enlargement of the bridgehead (7th - 18th June).
• The consolidation of the bridgehead (18st June - 8st July).
• The increase in military strength and the break-out, the "Cobra" offensive (25th-31st July).

The nature of the terrain, namely the Bocage, in what is called the Norman "Little Switzerland", where small fields are surrounded by high earth and stone banks topped by dense hedges and with often boggy area, favours defence. Neither offensive actions by the Allied armour, other Allied attacks nor enemy counter-attacks could reach any significant size. Bad weather hampered the landing of Allied supplies of both men and equipment. Throughout these two months, the Allies wore away at the German defences which exhausted themselves, without being able to throw the Allies back into the sea.

U.S. tanks in Cherbourg on the 27th June 1944.

AFTER THE 6TH JUNE: OPERATIONS AND THEIR CHRONOLOGY

BRITISH SECTOR	JUNE
• Airborne troops create bridgehead over the Orne	7
• Landing of the British 2nd Army and the Canadians	7
• Battle of the Odon and Operation Epsom	24
• Capture of Caen (Operations Charnwood and Atlantic)	
• Operations Goodwood and Spring	
• The break-out from the Bocage (Operation Bluecoat)	
• The push on Falaise (Operations Totalize and Tractable)	
THE AMERICAN SECTOR	
• Landing of the American 1st Army at Omaha and the airborne forces bridgehead	7 16
• The Cotentin Battle	18
• The war in the hedgerows of the Bocage	2
• The break-out, or Operation COBRA	
• The American pursuit, counter-attack and the German retreat in the Mortain-Argentan pocket	
THE END OF THE BATTLE	
• The Falaise pocket	

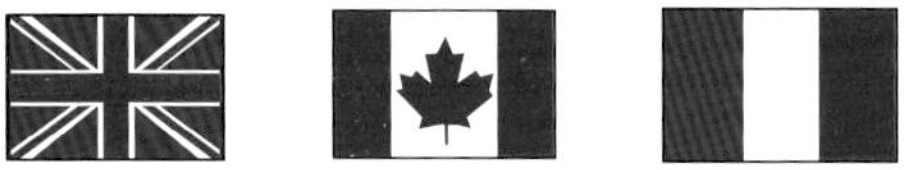

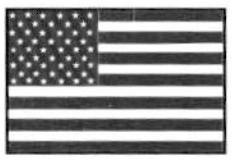

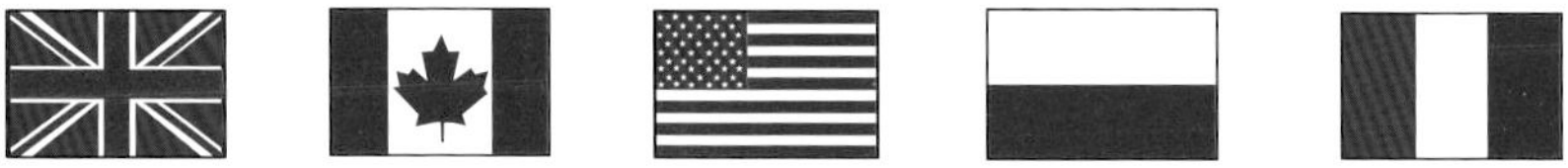

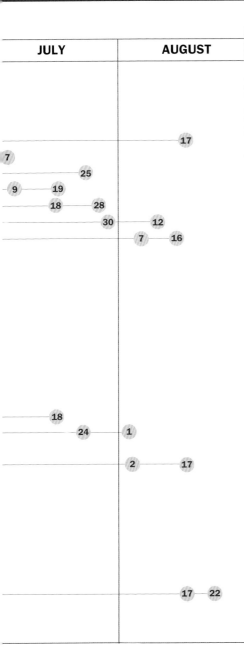

JULY	AUGUST

NAMES OF THE OPERATIONS AND THEIR OBJECTIVES

Operation Epsom
Operation launched by the British from West of Caen with the objective of securing a bridgehead on the river Odon

Operations Charnwood and Atlantic
Designed to clear the town of Caen and liberate the villages to the South West of Caen.

Operations Goodwood and Spring
The first was designed to attack the right bank of the Orne with 3 Armoured Divisions, with artillery and air support. The second was to clear the villages to the South of Caen and prepare a base for a subsequent push in the direction of Falaise.

Operation Bluecoat
A general offensive through the Bocage and support for Operation COBRA whose main objective was hill 309 overlooking Villers-Bocage.

Operations Totalize and Tractable
Launched by Montgomery, the first was designed to begin the encirclement of the German VIIth Army, South of Caen, with the help of the Canadian 1st Army. The second, with the Canadian 4th Division and the Polish 1st Division, was to hasten to the South in order to join up with the Americans and to reclose the gap through which the Germans were attempting to escape.

Operation Cobra
The push of the American 1st Army towards Avranches.

THE ENLARGEMENT from 6th June to 18th June 1944

The joining up of the landing beaches, the enlargement of the bridgehead

On the 7th of June, the Americans advanced slowly South of Omaha, always under fire from automatic weapons of many calibres, but some patrols pushed Eastwards to establish a first contact with the British troops near Port-en-Bessin. The situation at Omaha remained serious, but would shortly improve because the German 352nd Division, scarred by the battles of D-Day, had not received any reinforcements.

By the evening of the 8th June, the American bridgehead at Omaha had been extended to a depth of 10km. Whilst Grandcamp was still occupied by the Germans, the final link up of the American and British sectors was achieved West of Bayeux, which had been captured, undamaged, on the 7th by the British 56th Brigade.

Eisenhower and Bradley decided to try to unite the two bridgeheads at Utah and Omaha before trying to capture Cherbourg.

On the 9th, units of the American 5th Corps took Isigny and on the 10th, the forest of Cerisy. The same day, the 29th Division, coming from Omaha, and the 101st Airborne Division established a first link up while fierce fighting took place in the region of Montebourg to the North of Sainte-Mere-Eglise.

On the 12th June, the 101st Division, after a hard fight, managed to take Carentan, thus completing the unification of the bridgeheads. From Ouistreham in the East to Saint-Marcouf in the West, the Allies created a bridgehead 80km wide and 10 to 30km deep.

By the evening of 12th of June (D-Day + 6), there had been landed in the bridgehead, 16 Divisions, with 326,547 men, 3,186 vehicles and 104,428 tons of supplies. Of the 16 Divisions, 9 were American and 7 British and Canadian. On the same day, a gloomy Rommel summarised the situation: "*The enemy is being reinforced, under the umbrella of his air superiority... the enemy is being reinforced much more rapidly than our reserves can reach us... our position is extremely difficult. The enemy has complete air supremacy over the combat zones and up to 100km in the rear of them*"

Saint-Lô, 18th July 1944.

Montebourg, summer 1944.

By the 18th of June (D-Day +12), the Allied bridgehead had been enlarged sufficiently for Eisenhower and Montgomery to be able to define their next plan of action; this was to consolidate the bridgehead extending from the base of the Cotentin peninsular and the heights above St-Lô to   the hills North of Caen, and to make efforts to capture the port of Cherbourg and put pressure on Caen in order to attract enemy reserves to it.

THE CONSOLIDATION from 18th June to 18th July 1944

The developement and consolidation of the bridgehead

For the American 1st Army, the main objective to be achieved as quickly as possible was the Port of Cherbourg. The first attack was launched on the 22nd of June. Street fighting in Cherbourg took place on the 25th and 26th.

At 18.00 hours, the Commanders of the land and naval forces surrendered. Von Schlieben was taken prisoner, as was Admiral Hennecke, toget The recent storm that had raged and which was the cause of the destruction of the artificial harbour at St-Laurent and damage to that at Arromanches, had a profound impact on the tactical situation.

An attack, code named "EPSOM", to the West of Caen and planned for the 22nd, had to be put back to a later date. For the British 2nd Army, it was a question of causing as many German Divisions as possible to be kept in the East, whilst at the same time, trying to capture Caen.

Montgomery wanted to bring forward his offensive and capture Caen before any attack by Rommel could be mounted; this was the reason for laun ching "EPSOM".

The storm of the 19th June 1944 at Arromanches.

The storm of the 19th June 1944 at Arromanches.

On the 28th, a bridgehead was established on the far bank of the Odon.

On the 4th July, the Canadian 3rd Division engaged in a fierce battle for Carpiquet. Caen, squeezed between the salient West of the Odon and the pocket created to the East of the Orne on D-Day itself by the British 6th Airborne Division was, on the 1st July, considered by the German commanders to be untenable. At the end of June, German losses were assessed at 200,000 dead, wounded or taken prisoner, and the 7 Panzer Divisions involved lost more than 300 tanks.

On the 9th July, British and Canadian troops entered the ruins of Caen. The capture of Cherbourg and the occupation of the North of the Cotentin peninsular between the 26th and 30th June and the capture of the Northern part of Caen on the 9th July, marked the achievement of the objectives initially fixed for Overlord and the end of the period of consolidation of the bridgehead. To the rear of the now uninterrupted line from Cap Carteret (on the West coast of the Cotentin) to Caen, there could now take place reinforcement and regrouping with a view to an offensive drive into the heart of France.

General Joseph L. Collins, Commander of the 7th U.S. Army Corps at Le Fort du Roule in Cherbourg on June 27th 1944.

Fort du Roule today.

THE BREAKTHROUGH

from 8th July to 31th July 1944

The push towards the interior of France was preceded by an offensive opened on the 3rd of July by the American 8th Army Corps in the direction of St-Lô, the prior capture of which was judged to be necessary. There was fierce resistance at La Haye du Puits and St-Lô only fell on the 18th.

In the Anglo-Canadian sector, Operation Goodwood (an operation to encircle and capture Caen) met bitter resistance between the 18th and 24th July. 36 Tiger tanks played a vital role in this resistance. The British 11th Division lost 126 tanks in one day. Caen was completely liberated, but in ruins and the Caen plain cleared for 7km around the town. Montgomery, Commander in Chief of the Land forces, was satisfied with the result of the operation which opened up for him the roads South of Caen and had drawn the bulk of the German armour to the East, thus correspondingly freeing the Western part of the front to the benefit of Bradley and Operation COBRA, planned for the 20th July.

Caen, July 1944, clearing the rue de Bayeux, viewed from the Abbaye aux hommes.

▼ The armour of the 2nd Armoured Division under Leclerc assembling at Vesly, in the Manche Department, on 5th August 1944.

On 20th July, everything was in place for the opening of the COBRA offensive, but adverse weather conditions caused it to be postponed until the 25 of July. In the morning of the 25th, carpet bombing was carried out by 2,250 bombers, of which 1,500 were strategic bombers. This carpet bombing of objectives ensured the success of COBRA.

The American 4th Division pushed audaciously into the breach opened at Coutances. On the 30th, in the evening, it reached Avranches, over 50km further South. It succeeded in taking the bridge at Pontaubault, which opened the road to Brittany and the Loire. The break out had been achieved. Defying all rational expectations, over this one bridge, the only one in his possession, Patton passed 7 Divisions in 72 hours! One armoured Division set off towards Brest; Rennes was taken on the 4th of August, Angers on the 10th and Nantes on the 12th.

The 3rd Army, including the 2nd Armoured Division of General Leclerc, made up one part of the spearhead, but then drew back, so as to deceive the enemy, and executed a wide sweep to the East, reaching Le Mans on the 9th August. General Montgomery, for his part, launched his Divisions to the South and South East.

The Abbaye aux hommes.

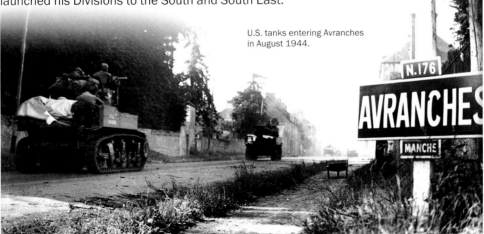

U.S. tanks entering Avranches in August 1944.

THE FALAISE POCKET from 31ᵗʰ July to 21ˢᵗ August 1944

'Panther' tank destroyed in the Falaise pocket in 1944.

The counter offensive, launched on the direct orders of Hitler himself, during the night of 6/7ᵗʰ August from Mortain, ended on the 17ᵗʰ with the annihilation of the panzers in the Falaise pocket.

The pocket had been shrinking day by day, under the weight of attacks by American, British and Canadian Divisions, as well as incessant aerial bombardment. On the 19th and 20th of August, the pocket became a furnace, a veritable "cauldron", from which the German units tried to extract themselves, abandoning their equipment.

In his report on the operation, Eisenhower summed up this final phase of the Battle of Normandy in the following words *"In the pocket itself, the enemy strategy consisted of siting his armour along its Southern edge, passing through Argentan, facing the Americans, and a strong defensive barrier at Falaise directed against the Canadians, with 21 Panzer Divisions and the 12th SS Panzer Division. By this means and by offering fierce resistance,*

Armour on the way to Chambois, after the liberation of Falaise on 17ᵗʰ July 1944.

the Germans managed to keep the jaws of our pincers separated for long enough to allow a proportion of their forces to escape."

The main German forces suffered a crushing defeat. Their losses reached 240,000 killed or wounded, 210,000 taken prisoner, 3,500 guns, 1,500 tanks and a large quantity of vehicles and equipment of all types. Thereafter, nothing could halt the spectacular advance of the Allied forces on the Seine and Paris. On the 25th of August, Paris was liberated. Less than 8 days afterwards, the Somme was crossed.

Falaise Church after the liberation of the town by the Canadians on 17th August 1944.

The battle of the Falaise pocket

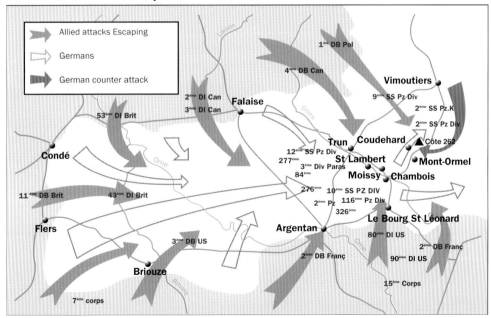

D-DAY IN FACTS AND FIGURES

NAVAL FORCES

Ships		Servicemen	
• Warships	138	• Sailors:	
• Destroyers, frigates, corvettes	221	British	
• Mine sweepers	287	𝍏	112,824
• Smaller vessels	495	American	
• Submarine chasers	58	𝍏	52,889
• Landing craft of all types	Over 4,000	other Allied servicemen	
• Auxiliary Naval craft and small boats	441	𝍏	4,988
• Merchant Navy ships	864	• Merchant navy:	
• Other small craft	Over 300	𝍏	25,000
In total, more than 6,800 vessels of which warships were:		**Total:**	**195,701**
– 79 % British			
– 16,5 % American			
– 4,5 % Other Allies			

AIR FORCES

Aircraft		Air crew	
• Aircraft of which	11,590	𝍏	31,000
5,510 British and Canadian, 6,080 American		(not including airborne troops or their aircrews)	
• Gliders	3,500		

LAND FORCES

Vehicles	Men			
20,000 (inc. rather over 1,000 tanks)	**Landed on the beaches**		**Troops parachuted or landed by glider**	
	American sector:	57,500	American	15,500
	(23,250 Utah and 34,250 Omaha)			
	British sector:	75,215	British and Canadian	7,990
	(24,970 Gold, 21,400 Juno and 28,845 Sword)			
	Total	**132,715**	**Total**	**24,490**

Total land forces deployed for D-Day: 157,205